NATIONAL FINANCES—SPECIE PAYMENTS.

SPEECH

OF

HON. JOHN SHERMAN,

OF OHIO,

IN THE

SENATE OF THE UNITED STATES,

MARCH 6, 1876.

WASHINGTON.
1876.

NATIONAL FINANCES—SPECIE PAYMENTS.

SPEECH

OF

HON. JOHN SHERMAN,

OF OHIO,

IN THE

SENATE OF THE UNITED STATES,

March 6, 1876.

WASHINGTON.
1876.

SPEECH

OF

HON. JOHN SHERMAN.

Mr. SHERMAN. I now move that the Senate proceed to the consideration of the motion to refer the resolutions of the Chamber of Commerce of the State of New York, relative to the national finances and in favor of the resumption of specie payments at the time now provided by law.

The PRESIDENT *pro tempore.* The Senator from Ohio moves that the Senate proceed to consider the motion to refer the resolutions of the Chamber of Commerce of New York.

The motion was agreed to.

OUGHT THE RESUMPTION ACT OF 1875 BE REPEALED?

Mr. SHERMAN. Mr. President, I have taken the unusual course of arresting the reference to the Committee of Finance of the memorial of the Chamber of Commerce of New York in order to discuss in an impersonal and non-partisan way one of the questions presented by that memorial, and one which now fills the public mind and must necessarily soon occupy our attention. That question is, "Ought the resumption act of 1875 be repealed?" The memorial strongly opposes such repeal, while other memorials, and notably those from the Boards of Trade of New York and Toledo, advocate it. These opposing views are supported in each House of Congress, and will, when our time is more occupied than now, demand our vote.

And, sir, we are forced to consider this question when the law it is proposed to repeal is only commencing to operate, now, three years before it can have full effect—during all which time its operation will be under your eye and within your power—and while the passions of men are heated by a presidential combat, when a grave question, affecting the interests of every citizen of the United States, will be influenced by motives entirely foreign to the merits of the proposition.

QUESTIONS NOT INVOLVED.

And the question presented is not as to the best means of securing the resumption of a specie standard, but solely whether the only measure that promises that result shall be repealed. We know there is a wide and honest diversity of opinion as to the agency and means to secure a specie standard. When any practicable scheme to that end is proposed I am ready to examine it on its merits; but we are not considering the best mode of doing the thing, but whether we will recede from the promise made by the law as it stands as well as refuse all means to execute that promise. If the law is deficient in any respect it is open to amendment. If the powers vested in the Secretary are not sufficient or you wish to limit or enlarge them, he is your servant, and you have but to speak and he obeys. It is not whether we will accumulate gold or greenbacks or convert our notes into bonds, nor whether the time to resume is too early or too late. All these are subjects of legislation. But the question now is whether we will repudiate the legislative declaration made in the act of 1875 to redeem the promise made and printed on the face of every United States note, a promise made in the midst of war, when our nation was struggling for existence, a promise renewed in March, 1869, in the most unequivocal language, and finally made specific as to time by the act of 1875.

And let us not deceive ourselves by supposing that those who oppose this repeal are in favor of a purely metallic currency to the exclusion of paper currency, for all intelligent men agree that every great commercial nation must have both: the one as the standard of value by which all things are measured, which daily measures your bonds and notes as it measures wheat, cotton, and land; and also a paper or credit currency, which, from its convenience of handling or transfer, must be the medium of exchanges in the great body of the business of life. Statistics show that in commercial countries a very large proportion of all transfers is by book-accounts and notes, and more than nine-tenths of all the residue of payments is by checks, drafts, and such paper tools of exchange. Of the vast business done in New York and London not 5 per cent. is done with either paper money or gold or silver, but by the mere balancing of accounts or exchange of credits. And this will be so whether your paper money is worth 40 per cent. or 100 per cent. in gold. The only question is whether in using paper money we will have that which is as good as it promises, as good as that of Great Britain, France, or Germany; as good as coin issued from your mints, or whether we will content ourselves with depreciated paper money, worth 10 per cent less than it promises, every dollar of which daily tells your constituents that the United States is not rich enough to pay more than 90 per cent. on the dollar for its three hundred and seventy millions of promises to pay, or that you have not courage enough to stand by your promise to do it.

Nor are we to decide whether our paper money shall be issued directly by the Government or by banks created by the Government; nor whether at a future time the legal-tender quality of United States notes shall continue. I am one of those who believe that a United States note issued directly by the Government and convertible on demand into gold coin, or a Government bond equal in value to gold, is the best currency we can adopt; that it is to be the currency of the future, not only in the United States, but in Great Britain as well; and that such a currency might properly continue to be a legal tender except when coin is specifically stipulated for.

But these are not the questions we are to deal with. It is whether the promise of the law shall be fulfilled, that the United States shall pay such of its notes as are presented on and after the 1st day of January, 1879, in coin; and whether the national banks will at the same time redeem their notes either in coin or United States notes made equal to coin; or whether the United States shall revoke its promise and continue for an indefinite period to still longer force upon the people a depreciated currency always below the legal standard of gold, and fluctuating daily in its depreciation as Congress may threaten or promise, or speculators may hoard, or corner, or throw out your broken promises. It is the turning point in our financial history, which will greatly affect the life of individuals and the fate of parties, but, more than all, the honor and good faith of our country.

At the beginning of our national existence our ancestors boldly and hopefully assumed the burden of a great national debt, formed of the debts of the old confederation and of the States that composed it;

and, with a scattered population and feeble resources, honestly met and paid in good solid coin every obligation. After the war of 1812, which exhausted our resources, destroyed our commerce, and greatly increased our debt, a republican administration boldly funded our debt, placed its currency upon the coin basis, promptly paid its interest, and reduced the principal; and within twenty years after that war was over, under the first democratic President, paid in coin the last dollar, both principal and interest, of the debt. And now, eleven years after a greater war, of grander proportions, in which not merely foreign domination threatened us, but the very existence of our nation was at stake, and after our cause has been blessed with unexampled success, with a country teeming with wealth, with our credit equal to that of any nation, we are debating whether we will redeem our promises according to their legal tenor and effect, or whether we will refuse to do so and repeal and cancel them.

I would invoke in the consideration of this question the example of those who won our independence and preserved it to us, to inspire us so to decide this question that those who come after us may point to our example of standing by the public faith now solemnly pledged, even though to do so may not run current with the temporary pressure of the hour or may entail some sacrifice and hardship.

THE VITAL OBJECT OF THE ACT OF 1875.

What then is the law it is proposed to repeal? I will state its provisions fully in detail, but the main proposition—the essential core of the whole—is the promise to which the public faith is pledged that the United States will redeem in gold coin any of its notes that may be presented to the Treasury on and after the 1st day of January, 1879. This is the vital object of the law. It does not undertake to settle the nature of our paper money after that, whether it shall be reissued again, whether it shall thereafter be a legal tender, nor whether it shall or shall not supersede bank-notes. All this is purposely left to the future. But it does say that on and after that day the United States note promising to pay one dollar shall be equal to the gold dollar of the Mint.

The questions then arise—

First. Ought this promise be performed?

Second. Can we perform it?

Third. Are the agencies and measures prescribed in the law sufficient for the purpose?

Fourth. If not, what additional measures should be enacted?

Let us consider these questions in their order with all serious deliberation that their conceded importance demands.

And first, ought this promise be fulfilled?

THE LEGAL PURPORT OF UNITED STATES NOTES.

To answer this we must fully understand the legal and moral obligations contained in the notes of the United States. The purport of the note is as follows:

> The United States promises to pay the bearer one dollar.

This note is a promise to pay one dollar. The legal effect of this note has been announced by the unanimous opinion of the Supreme Court of the United States, the highest and final judicial authority in our Government.

The legal-tender attribute given to the note has been the subject of conflicting decisions in that court, but the nature and purport of it is not only plain on its face, but is concurred in by every judge of that court and by every judicial tribunal before which that question has been presented.

In the case of Bank *vs.* Supervisors, 7 Wallace, 31, Chief Justice Chase says:

But, on the other hand, it is equally clear that these notes are obligations of the United States. Their name imports obligation. Every one of them expresses upon its face an engagement of the nation to pay to the bearer a certain sum. The dollar note is an engagement to pay a dollar, and the dollar intended is the *coined* dollar of the United States, a certain quantity in weight and fineness of gold or silver, authenticated as such by the stamp of the Government. No other dollars had before been recognized by the legislation of the National Government as lawful money.

Again, in the case of Bronson *vs.* Rhodes, 7 Wallace, 251, Chief Justice Chase says:

The note dollar was the promise to pay a coined dollar.

In the Legal-Tender Cases, 12 Wallace, 560, Justice Bradley says:

It is not an attempt to *coin* money out of a valueless material, like the coinage of leather, or ivory, or cowry shells. *It is a pledge of the national credit.* It is a *promise* by the Government to *pay dollars;* it is not an attempt to *make* dollars. The standard of value is not changed. The Government simply demands that its credit shall be accepted and received by public and private creditors during the pending exigency. * * *

No one supposes that these Government certificates are never to be paid; that the day of specie payments is never to return. And it matters not in what form they are issued. * * * Through whatever changes they pass, their ultimate destiny is *to be* paid.

In all these legal-tender cases there is not a word in conflict with these opinions.

Thus, then, it is settled that this note is not a dollar, but a debt due; a promise to pay a dollar in gold coin. Congress may define the weight and fineness of a dollar, and it has done so by providing a gold coin weighing $25\frac{8}{10}$ grains of standard gold $\frac{9}{10}$ fine. The promise is specific and exact, and its nature is fixed by the law and announced by the court. Here I might rest as to the nature of the United States note; but it is proper that I state the law under which it was issued and the subsequent laws relating to it.

The act of February 25, 1862, gave birth to this note as well as the whole financial policy of the war. The first section of that act authorizes the Secretary of the Treasury to issue upon the credit of the United States, United States notes to the amount of $150,000,000, payable to bearer at the Treasury of the United States. The amount of these notes was subsequently increased during the war to the maximum sum of $450,000,000, but the nature and character of the notes was the same as the first issue. The enlargement of the issue did not in the least affect the obligation of the United States to pay them in coin. This obligation was recognized in every loan law passed during the war; and to secure the note from depreciation the amount was carefully limited, and every quality was given to it to maintain its value that was possible during the exigencies of the war. I might show you from the contemporaneous debates in Congress that at every step of the war the notes were regarded as a temporary loan, in the nature of a forced loan, but a loan cheerfully borne, and to be redeemed soon after the war was over. It was not until two years after the war, when the advancing value of the note created an interest to depreciate it in order to advance prices for purposes of speculation, that there was any talk about putting off the payment of the note. The policy of a gradual contraction of the currency with a view to specie payments was in December, 1865, concurred in by the almost unanimous vote of the House of Representatives, and the act of April 12, 1866, authorized $4,000,000 of notes a month to be retired and canceled. No one then questioned either the policy, the duty, or the obligation of the United States to redeem these notes in coin.

WHY THE UNITED STATES NOTE IS BELOW PAR.

Why has not this obligation been performed? How comes it that fourteen years after these notes were issued, and eleven years after the exigency was over, we are debating whether they shall be paid and when they shall be paid? We may well pause to examine how this plain and positive obligation has so long been deferred by a nation always sensitive to the public honor.

The fatal commencement of this long delay was in this provision of the act approved March 3, 1863, as follows:

And the holders of United States notes issued under and by virtue of said acts shall present the same for the purpose of exchanging the same for bonds as therein provided on or before the 1st day of July, 1863, and thereafter the right so to exchange the same shall cease and determine.

Thus, under the pressure of war and the plausible pretext of a statute of limitations, the most essential legal attribute of the note was taken away. This act, though convenient in its temporary results, was a most fatal step, and for my part in acquiescing in and voting for it I have felt more regret than for any act of my official life. But it must be remembered that the object of this provision was not to prevent the conversion of notes into bonds, but to induce their conversion. It was the policy and need of the Government to induce its citizens to exchange the notes freely for the bonds, so that the notes might again be paid out to meet the pressing demands of the war. It was believed that if this right to convert them was limited, in time this would cause them to be more freely funded; and Mr. Chase, then Secretary of the Treasury, anxious to prevent a too large increase of the interest of the public debt, desired to place in market a 5 per cent. bond instead of a 6 per cent. bond. The fatal error was in not changing the right to convert the note into a 5 per cent. bond instead of a 6 per cent. bond. This was in fact proposed in the Committee on Finance, but it was said that a right to convert a note into a bond at any time was not so likely to be exercised as if it could only be exercised at the pleasure of the Government. And this plausible theory to induce the conversion of notes into bonds was made the basis after the war was over for the refusal of the United States to allow the conversion of its notes into bonds, and has been the fruitful cause of the continued depreciation and dishonor of United States notes for the last five years, during which our 5 per cent. bonds have been at par with gold, while our notes rise and fall in the gamut of depreciation from 6 to 22 per cent. below gold.

Notwithstanding that the right to convert notes into bonds was taken away, yet in fact they were during the war received par for par for bonds; and after the war was over all the interest-bearing securities were converted into bonds; but the notes—the money of the people—the artificial measure of value, the most sacred obligation, because it was past due, was refused either payment or conversion, thus cutting it off from the full benefit of the advancing credit of the Government, and leaving to it only the forced quality of legal tender in payment of debts.

Shortly after the war was over, and notably during the presidential campaign of 1868, the question arose whether the bonds of the United States were payable in coin or United States notes. Both notes and bonds were then below par in coin, the notes ranging from sixty-seven to seventy-five cents in coin; and 5 per cent. bonds from seventy-two to eighty cents in coin. Here again the opportunity was lost to secure the easy and natural appreciation of our notes to the gold standard. Had Congress then authorized the conversion of notes into bonds when both were depreciated both would have advanced to par in gold; but on the one hand it was urged that this would cause a rapid contraction, and on the other that the right to convert the note into a bond was not specie payment; it was only the exchange of one promise for another. It was specie payment they very much favored, but did not have the wisdom then to secure. If the advocates for specie payment had then supported a restoration of the right to convert notes into bonds they would have secured their object with but little opposition. But all measures to fund the notes at the pleasure of the holder were defeated, and instead there was ingrafted into the act to strengthen the public credit—

First, a declaration "that the faith of the United States is solemnly pledged to the payment in coin, or its equivalent, of all the obligations of the United States not bearing interest, known as United States notes, and of all the interest-bearing obligations of the United States" except such as by the law could be paid in other currency than gold and silver.

Second, "and the United States also solemnly pledges its faith to make provision, at the earliest practicable period, for the redemption of the United States notes in coin."

Here again the obligation of the Government to pay these notes in coin was recognized, its purpose declared, and the time fixed, "as early as practicable." What was the effect of this important act of Congress? Without adding one dollar to the public debt, or the burden of the debt, both bonds and notes rose in value. Within one year the bonds rose to par in gold, making it practicable to commence the refunding of 6 per cent. bonds into 5 per cent bonds. The notes rose under the stimulus of this new promise in one year from seventy-six cents to eighty-nine cents in gold, but no steps whatever were made to redeem them.

The amount of bank-notes authorized was increased fifty-four millions. The executive department pursued the policy of redeeming debts not due, and did from an overflowing Treasury reduce very largely the public debt, but no steps whatever were taken to advance the value of our notes. The effect of the act of 1869 was exhausted on the adjournment of Congress in March, 1870, when the United States notes were worth eighty-nine cents in gold; and thereabouts, up and down, with many fluctuations, they have remained to this day. The bondholder, secure in the promise to him, is happy in receiving his interest in gold, with his bond above par in gold. The note-holder, the farmer, the artisan, the laborer, whose labor and production is measured in greenbacks, still receives your depreciated notes worth 10 per cent. less than gold you promised him "at the earliest day practicable." The one has a promise performed and the other a promise postponed.

Thus we stood when the panic of '73 came upon us; with more paper money afloat than ever circulated before in any country of the world. Even then, had we stood firmly, the hoarding tendency of the panic would have advanced our notes toward the gold standard, and in fact did so during the months of September and October, until the premium on gold had fallen to 8 per cent. But sir, at this critical moment, the Secretary of the Treasury, acting no doubt in good faith, but I think without authority of law, issued twenty-six millions more United States notes—part of the notes retired and canceled under previous acts. And now, notwithstanding all the talk about contraction of the currency, we have not withdrawn one-half of this illegal issue. On the 1st of September, 1873, we had three hundred and fifty-six million notes outstanding. Three months afterward we had three hundred and eighty-two million; and now we have three hundred and seventy-one million.

THE ACT OF 1875 A PLEDGE OF PUBLIC FAITH.

Sir, it was under the light of these events, after the fullest discussion ever given in Congress of any question—after debate before the people during the recess of Congress and full deliberation last winter—this act was passed. There was and is now great difference of opinion as to the details, but the vital promise made to the note-holder to make his note as good as gold in January, 1879, was concurred in by a large majority of both Houses, and by many who opposed the bill as too slow in its operations. This act of honor and public faith was applauded by the civilized world and concurred in by our constituents, the doubts only being as to the machinery to carry it into effect. The time was fixed by those who most feared resumption, and no one proposed a longer time. My honorable friend from Indiana [Mr. MORTON] truly said (in the recent campaign in Ohio) that he participated in framing it; and he and those who agreed with him fixed the time so remote as to excite the unfounded charge that the bill was a sham, a mere contrivance to bridge an election.

And now, sir, to recapitulate this branch of the question, it is shown that the holder of these notes has a promise of the United States made in February, 1862, to pay him $1 in gold coin; that the legal purport of this promise has been declared by the Supreme Court; that we have taken away from this note one of the legal attributes given it which would long since have secured its payment in coin—that when the note was authorized and issued it was understood as redeemable in coin when the war was over; that our promise to pay it was renewed in 1869—"at as early a day as practicable;" that by reason of our failure to provide for its payment it is still depreciated below par more than one-tenth of its nominal value; that we renewed this promise and made it definite as to time by act of 1875; that it is a debt due from the United States, and in law and honor due now in coin. Yet it is proposed to recall our promise to redeem this note in coin three years hence. I say, sir, this would be national dishonor. It would destroy the confidence with which the public creditor rests upon the promises contained in your bonds. It would greatly tend to arrest the process by which the interest on your bonds is reduced. It would accustom our people to the substitution of a temporary wave of popular opinion for its written contract or promise. It would weaken in the public mind that keen sense of honor and pride which has always distinguished the English-speaking nations in dealing with public obligations.

An old writer thus describes "public credit:"

> Credit is a consequence, not a cause; the effect of a substance, not a substance; it is the sunshine, not the sun; the quickening *something*, call it what you will, that gives life to trade, gives being to the branches and moisture to the root; it is the oil of the wheel, the marrow in the bones, the blood in the veins, and the spirits in the heart of all the negoce, trade, cash, and commerce in the world.
>
> It is produced, and grows insensibly from fair and upright dealing, punctual compliance, honorable performance of contracts and covenants; in short, it is the offspring of universal probity.
>
> It is apparent even by its nature; it is no way dependent upon persons, parliament, or any particular men or set of men as such in the world, but upon their conduct and just behavior. Credit never was chained to men's names, but to their

actions; not to families, clans, or collections of men; no, not to nations. It is the honor, the justice, the fair-dealing, and the equal conduct of men, bodies of men, nations, and people, that raise the thing called credit among them. Wheresoever this is found credit will live and thrive, grow and increase; where this is wanting, let all the power and wit of man join together, they can neither give her being nor preserve her life.

Arts have been tried on various occasions in the world to raise credit; art has been found able with more ease to destroy credit than to raise it. The force of art, assisted by the punctual, fair, and just-dealing abovesaid, may have done much to form a credit upon the face of things, but we find still the honor would have done it without the art, but never the art without the honor. Nor will money itself, which, Solomon says, answers all things, purchase this thing called credit or restore it when lost. * * *

Our credit in this case is a public thing. It is rightly called by some of our writers *national credit.* The word denominates its original. It is produced by the nation's probity, the honor and exact performing national engagements.

WHY PUBLIC POLICY FORBIDS ITS REPEAL.

And, sir, passing from considerations of public honor, there are many reasons of *public policy* which forbid the repeal of the act of 1875. That act was generally regarded as the settlement of a financial policy by which at least the party in power is bound, and upon the faith of which business men have conducted their affairs and made their contracts. Debts have been contracted and paid with the expectation that at the time fixed the gold standard would measure all obligations, and a repeal of the act would now re-open all the wild and dangerous speculation schemes that feed and fatten upon depreciated paper money. The influence that secures this repeal will not stop here. If we can recall our promise to pay our notes outstanding why should we not issue more? If we can disregard our promise to pay them, why shall we regard our promise not to issue more than $400,000,000 as stipulated for by the act of 1864? If we can re-open the question of the payment of our notes, why may we not re-open the question as to the payment of our bonds? Is the act of 1869 any more sacred than the act of 1875? And if we can re-open these questions, why not re-open the laws requiring the payment of either interest or principal of the public debt? They rest upon acts of Congress which we have the power to repeal. If the public honor cannot protect our promise to the note-holder, how shall it protect our promise to the bondholder? Already do we see advocated in high places, by numerous and formidable organizations, all forms of repudiation, which, if adopted, would reduce our nation to the credit of a robber chief—worse than the credit of an Algerine pirate, who at least would not plunder his own countrymen. And if the public creditor had no safety, what chance would the national banks—creations of our own and subject to our will—have in Congress? It has already been proposed to confiscate their bonds, premium and all, as a mode of paying their notes with greenbacks. What expedient so easy if we would make money cheap and abundant? Or, if so extreme a measure could be arrested, what is to prevent the permanent dethronement of gold as a measure of value, and the substitution of an interconvertible currency bond bearing 3.65 per cent. interest as a standard of value; and when it becomes too expensive to print the notes to pay the interest, reduce the rate. Why not? Why pay 3.65 per cent. when it is easier to print 3? It is but an act of Congress. And when the process of repudiation goes so far that your notes will not buy bread, why then declare against all interest, and then, after passing through the valley of humiliation return again to barter, and honor, and gold again.

Sir, if you once commence this downward course of repudiation there is but one ending. You may, like Mirabeau and the Girondists.

seek to stem the torrent, but you will be swept away by the spirit you have evoked and the instruments you have created. You complain now of a want of confidence which makes men hoard their money. Will you, then, destroy *all* confidence? No, sir, no; the way to *restore* confidence is to *inspire* it by fulfilling your obligations. You cannot make men lend you; you cannot make men sell you anything—either bread, or meat, or wool, or iron, or anything that is or that can be created—except for that which they choose to take. You may depreciate the money which you offer, but it will only take more of it to buy what you want. It is true that the creditor may, by your laws, be compelled to take your money however much you depreciate it, but he cannot buy back that which he sold, or its equivalent in other necessaries of life, and thus he is cheated of part of what he sold. During the war, while money was depreciating, many a simple man gleefully counted his gains as he sold his goods or crops at advancing prices, but he found out his mistake when with his swollen pile he tried to replace his stock in trade or laid in his supplies. Sir, this policy exhausts itself in cheating the man who buys or sells or loans on credit, who produces something to sell on credit; whether that something be food or clothing; whether it be a necessity or a luxury of life. Productive labor, honest toil, whether of the farmer or the artisan, is deeply interested in credit. It is credit that gives life and competition to trade; and credit is destroyed by every scheme that impairs, delays, or even clouds an obligation.

Again, sir, an irredeemable and fluctuating currency always raises the rate of interest on money, while a stable currency or an improving currency always reduces the rate of interest. This is easily shown by statistics, but the reason is so obvious that proof is not needed. If a man lends his money he wants it back again with its increase; but if the money, when it is to be paid back, is like to be worth less than when he thinks of loaning it, he will not loan it except at such rates as will cover the risk of depreciation. He will prefer to buy land or something of stable value. If money is at the gold standard or is advancing toward that standard, he will loan it readily at a moderate interest, for he knows he will receive back money of at least equal value to that he loaned.

Again, sir, with a depreciated currency great domestic productions are cut off from the foreign market; for it is impossible that with such a currency we can compete on equal terms with rival nations, whose industry rests upon a specie standard. As we approach such a standard, we are now able as to a few articles to compete with foreign industry; but it is only as to articles in the manufacture of which we have peculiar advantages. Let us rest our industries on that standard, and soon we could compete in the markets of the world in all the articles produced from iron, wood, leather, and cotton, the raw basis of which are our natural productions. And it must be remembered that all the countries with which we compete are specie-paying countries. A country that does not rest her industry upon specie is necessarily excluded from the great manufacturing industries of modern civilization, and is self-condemned to produce only the raw basis for advanced industry. Cheap food, climate, soil, or natural advantages, such as cheap land, vast plains for pasture, or rich mines, may give to a country wealth and prosperity in spite of the evils of depreciated paper money; but when we come in competition with the world in the advanced grades of production which give employment to the skilled mechanic, we must rest such industry upon the gold basis, or we enter the lists like a knight with his armor unbound.

Again, sir, a depreciated and fluctuating currency is a premium and bounty to the broker and money-changer. Under his manipulation our paper standard of value goes up and down, and he gambles and speculates, with all the advantages in his favor. Good people look on and think that it is gold that is going up and down; that their money is a dollar still, and trade and traffic in that belief. But the shrewd operator calculates daily the depreciation of our note, the shortening of the yard-stick, the shrinkage of the acre, the lessening of the ton, and thus it is that he daily adds to his gains from the indifference or delusion of our people.

Sir, it is an old story, often repeated in our day, and most eloquently epitomized by Daniel Webster in the often-quoted passage of his speech in which he said:

> A disordered currency is one of the greatest of political evils. It undermines the virtues necessary for the support of the social system and encourages propensities destructive of its happiness. It wars against industry, frugality, and economy: and it fosters the evil spirit of extravagance and speculation. Of all contrivances for cheating the laboring classes of mankind none has been more effectual than that which deluded them with paper money. Ordinary tyranny, oppression, excessive taxation, these bear lightly on the happiness of the mass of the community, compared with the fraudulent currencies and the robberies committed by depreciated paper. Our own history has recorded for our instruction enough, and more than enough, of the demoralizing tendency, the injustice, and the intolerable oppression of the virtuous and well-disposed of a degraded paper currency authorized by law or in any way countenanced by Government.

Sir, we must meet this question of specie payments, not only because the public honor is pledged to do so, but also for the lesser reason that it is our interest to do so. The only questions we should permit ourselves to discuss are the means and measures of doing so.

And now, sir, let us examine the reasons that have been given for the repeal of the resumption act by those who, though favoring resumption, yet think the act should be repealed for one or other of the following reasons:

First. That it is not advisable to fix a day for resumption.

Second. Or at least until the balance of trade is in our favor.

Third. That it produces a contraction of the currency.

Fourth. That it injuriously adds to the burden of existing debts.

Let us glance at these objections.

WHY FIX A DAY FOR RESUMPTION.

First. As to fixing a day for resumption.

If it was possible to agree upon measures that would secure resumption without fixing a time, I agree it would not be indispensable, though not unadvisable, to fix a time; but such agreement is utterly impossible. Of the multitude of schemes that have been presented to me by intelligent men trying to solve this problem, many could have been selected that in my opinion would be practicable; but of all of them not one ever has or is likely to secure the assent of a majority of a body so numerous as Congress. One difficulty we have encountered is that the democratic party, though in the minority, has never presented in any form through any leading member a plan for resumption, but with widely differing opinions have joined in opposing any and every measure from the other side. I understand from the papers that our democratic friends through a caucus, and through a caucus committee of which my colleague is chairman, have been laboring to agree upon a plan for specie payments. After his frequent speeches to us about a caucus measure—a great question being submitted to a caucus—about secret conclaves, about shams and deceptions and such like polite and friendly comments upon the work of the republican party, I might greet my colleague with such happy phrases about *his* caucus; but I will not, but on the contrary I commend his labors, and sincerely hope that he and his political friends may agree upon some plan to reach a specie standard, and not one to avoid it, to prevent it, to defer it. Under color of intending to prepare for it, I hope they will not make their measure the pretext for repealing the law as it stands, which fixes a day for resumption and will secure the end we both aim at.

I frankly state for the republican party that, while we could agree to fixing the time for specie payments and upon conferring the ample and sufficient powers upon the Secretary of the Treasury contained in this law, we could not agree in prescribing the precise mode in which the process should be executed. Nor, in my opinion, was it at all essential that we should. Much must be left to the discretion of the officer charged with the execution of such a law. The powers conferred, as I shall show hereafter, are ample; and the discretion given will be exercised under the eye of Congress.

And, sir, there is strong force in the fact that in every example we have of the successful resumption of specie payments in this and other countries a fixed day has been named by legislative authority, and the details and power of execution have been left to executive authority. Thus in Great Britain the act of Parliament of July 2, 1819, fixed the time for full resumption at the 1st day of May, 1823, and for a graduated resumption in gold at intermediate dates; and for fractional sums under forty shillings to be paid in silver coin; and the governor and directors of the Bank of England were charged with its execution, and authorized at their discretion to resume payment in full on the 1st day of May, 1822. France is now successfully passing through the same process of resumption, the time being fixed (two years ago) for January 1, 1878, and now practically attained. In our own country many of the States have presented similar laws in case of suspended bank payments, and in some cases the suspended banks have, by associated action, fixed a time for general resumption, and each bank adopted its own expedient for it. Sir, the light of experience is the lamp of wisdom. I can recall no case of successful resumption where a fixed future time has not been presented beforehand, either by law or agreement; while the historical examples of repudiation of currency have come by the drifting process, by a gradual decline of value, by increased issues, and a refusal to provide measures of redemption, until the whole mass disappeared, dishonored and repudiated.

This concurrence in the mode of resumption by so many governments was the strongest possible instruction to Congress when fixing a plan of resumption for the United States, and should satisfy reasonable men of its wisdom.

Besides, it would seem to be but fair that every one should have plain notice of so important a fact. If the measures only were presented and no time fixed it would be a matter of speculation, and the discretionary powers of the Secretary of the Treasury could be exercised with a view to hasten or postpone the time to the injury of individuals.

As to the date selected, I can only repeat it was placed as remote as any one suggested; far more so than is necessary to secure the object, and so that the fluctuations of value will scarcely exceed in four years what they have frequently been in a single year. An ample time to arrange all the relations of debtor and creditor, and to enable Congress to provide any additional measure in aid of resumption, or if events make it expedient to postpone the time.

BALANCE OF TRADE.

Again, it has been objected that we connot resume until the balance of trade is in our favor. This phrase, "balance of trade," has been a favorite one with visionaries and theorists, sufficiently indefinite to confuse and to mislead. As generally understood, the dogma is "that a nation that imports more than it exports is growing poorer;" or, conversely, "that a nation that exports more than it imports is prosperous." Now, sir, either proposition has been proven false in many cases, and may be true in some. It does not follow that an excess of imports creates distress, or a deficiency of exports is an evidence of poverty. Even the excess of imports upon which interest may be paid may be of wealth-producing productions, or a deficiency of exports may be caused by an increased domestic manufacture of raw products by home industry. But the best way to test the fallacy of this dogma is by reference to examples. Great Britain is known to be a prosperous nation of accumulating and accumulated wealth, and yet her imports have exceeded her exports every year for twenty years. The general average of her imports in excess of exports is £50,000,000 or $250,000,000 a year. I have here the detailed statement of her imports and exports for 1872 and 1873:

1872.	Imports	£354, 693, 624	
	Exports	314, 588, 834	
	Excess of imports over exports	40, 104, 790	or $200, 000, 000
1873.	Imports	371, 287, 372	
	Exports	311, 004, 765	
	Excess of imports over exports	60, 282, 607	or $300, 000, 000

Now, according to the dogma of the "balance of trade," Great Britain is going into a rapid decay; while she knows this large excess of imports is an addition to her national wealth.

But take our own country and compare years of conceded prosperity with years of hard times.

	1867.	1868.
Imports	$391, 121, 801	$351, 214, 010
Exports at gold value, including gold	334, 350, 653	352, 788, 202
Balance of trade against us	56, 771, 148	....

Yet we were then prosperous, as we have so often been told, with plenty of paper money.

Take the two last years, when we are told so often that distress, misery, and poverty prevailed:

	1874.	1875.
Exports at gold value, including gold	$652, 913, 445	$605, 574, 853
Imports	595, 861, 248	553, 906, 153
Balance of trade in our favor	57, 052, 197	51, 668, 700

And the balance of trade in our favor is more striking during the seven months of the present fiscal year, from the 1st of July, 1875, to the 1st of February, 1876.

The total exports, reduced to gold values, were	$334,853,996
The total imports were	281,729,735
Leaving a balance in our favor in coin for seven months of	53,124,261

All these amounts are reduced to a coin basis, and include both the importation and exportation of coin.

According to the dogma of the balance of trade, now is the golden moment to resume, when the balance is in our favor nearly one hundred millions a year. Yet many people cry out, "Wait for the balance of trade; don't force resumption." Well, the time has come, and yet they are not ready. This dogma has been the cause of infinite confusion, but is now abandoned. McCullough, in his Dictionary of Commerce, thus refers to it:

In commerce the term "balance of trade" is commonly used to express the difference between the value of the exports from and imports into a country. The balance *used* to be said to be favorable when the value of the exports exceeded that of the imports, and unfavorable when the value of the imports exceeded that of the exports. And in this country this was long believed to be the case, and down to a late period we were annually congratulated by our finance ministers on the excess of the exports over the imports.

The attainment of a favorable balance was formerly regarded as an object of the greatest importance. * * *

The truth is, however, that the theory of the balance of trade was not erroneous merely from the false notions which its advocates entertained with respect to money, but proceeded on radically mistaken views as to the nature of commerce. * * *

The argument about the balance of payments is one of those that contradict and confute themselves. * * *

Not only, therefore, is the theory with respect to the balance of trade erroneous, but the very reverse of that theory is true. * * *

It is difficult to estimate the mischief which the absurd notions relative to the balance of trade have occasioned in almost every commercial country; here they have been particular' injurious.

This author fortifies his position with ample details, but it is sufficient to say that if the dogma is false we should not regard it, and, if it is true, now is the golden moment for resumption, for the balance of trade is in our favor. In my view it is utterly immaterial to the question before us.

CONTRACTION.

The third objection is that the law produces a great contraction of the currency.

Now, sir, it ought to be confessed, for it is true, that any plan for specie resumption will, when it is about to take effect, produce some contraction of the paper currency. The drifting process if it succeeds must cause it as well. To wait for resumption until resumption will produce no temporary contraction is to wait until the rivers cease to flow or the mountains are level with the plains. Every time resumption has taken place in the historical cases I have referred to, contraction has preceded it. Remedies for bodily or political ailments are apt to be unpleasant. All we can say is that public honor and public policy demand the remedy for the dishonor and the evil of a depreciated currency; that the time is ripe for the cure and the means we have prescribed are suitable to the end.

And, sir, the degree of contraction and the effects of it are greatly exaggerated. The only contraction of the currency provided for by the act is in the substitution of one form of currency for another. Thus, in place of the fractional currency is issued silver currency; and where national-bank notes are issued there is retired 80 per cent. of the amount in United States notes. Thus far no fractional currency has been retired; but, as I will show hereafter, we can now and will, if the law stands, issue as much silver currency as any one may wish in exchange for either fractional currency or United States notes; and, as to bank-notes, the amount issued since the act took effect is $13,820,760, and the amount of United States notes retired is $11,056,608, leaving of United States notes still outstanding $370,943,-392, or $14,900.000 more than was outstanding when the act of March, 1869, was passed, and the same amount more than was outstanding on the 14th day of September, 1873, when the panic came. Thus it appears that under the law the amount of bank-notes issued is $2,800,000 more than the United States notes retired, and the contraction of the currency prescribed by this law is a myth.

But there has been a contraction of the currency since the panic, and before and after the passage of the act of 1875, which will go on whenever in any way a specie standard approaches, and that is by the voluntary retirement by national banks of a portion of their circulating notes. This contraction is not provided for by the resumption act, but is authorized by the national banking acts, and is the healthy ebb and flow of currency which it was the object of the law to secure. The national banks retired $24,962,327 of their notes by depositing that amount of United States notes in the Treasury of the United States to be used exclusively in redeeming the bank-notes when presented. The only motive for this deposit was that in the opinion of those banks the circulating notes could not be profitably used, or they were not strong enough to maintain at the specie basis the whole of their notes. This process will and ought to go on until each bank is certain it can maintain resumption at the time stated. Nor is this contraction in the slightest degree injurious to the bank or to the ability of the bank to loan money to its customers. The banks will not withdraw their notes unless it is their interest to do so. When they do surrender or redeem their notes they at once receive a larger amount of their bonds held as security for their notes, and worth about 30 per cent. more than the notes redeemed. Thus, when a bank surrenders $9,000 of its circulating notes it lifts from the lien of the note-holder $10,000 of United States bonds worth today about $12,000. If the bank sells the bonds it has $12,000 of currency to loan, and has strengthened itself by paying $9,000 of its notes. This process, instead of being a cause of alarm, should be encouraged and hastened; and this is practically the only contraction effected by this bill, a contraction which is in the very line clamored for by those who oppose national banks; but a voluntary contraction, made by the silent operation of the interest of the bank, while at the same time it advances the residue of notes to par in gold.

RESUMPTION THROUGH NATIONAL BANKS.

Sir, in my judgment, the real solution of specie resumption will thus come through the voluntary act of national banks, each acting for itself, under the general direction of the law, precisely as the Bank of England, the Bank of France, and the New York banks brought about and maintained resumption. I have never regarded with solicitude the amount of United States notes outstanding, for, as I will show, they can be easily maintained at par in gold; but the agency of the banks in securing resumption and the effect of resumption upon their customers were matters of solicitude. This I no longer doubt or fear. The whole problem consists in a partial and limited transfer of capital now invested by national banks in United States bonds to individuals. The high price of these bonds and the idle capital that seeks investment in them will enable each bank to strengthen itself by a sale of bonds without in the least impairing its ability to discount or loan, and, in fact, to increase its power to do so, and the bonds will be absorbed by the increasing demand for such securities. Strong banks in cities do not need the currency, for their currency is certified checks. Their currency is largely held by them, or, if in circulation, it can be retired and canceled without impairing in the least their ability to loan or discount. The bank currency being thus diminished, as the time for resumption approaches, the United States notes, supported by a gold reserve and the power of the Secretary to sell bonds, will easily be maintained at the gold standard, and the problem is solved.

And, sir, this partial contraction of bank currency will unlock and dissipate a greater contraction which has gone on since the panic, and will go on until the public mind rests assured that the day of resumption is not only promised but rendered certain by the course of events. An increase of currency will follow resumption. Great masses of notes now lie idle in bank-vaults and in the Treasury, and are hoarded in homesteads all over the land. There is deposited in the Treasury, without interest and belonging to banks, $31,005,000, represented by currency certificates. There are now in the vaults of the national banks $73,626,100 United States notes and fractional currency, $17,166,190 bank-notes, in all $90,792,290, and in the savings-banks, State banks, and other banks that have made returns to the Comptroller of the Currency the sum of $48,431,409, in all making $170,228,699, and this is far more than the reserve required by law. The practice of hoarding currency has greatly increased from the day of the panic, and it may be safely said that there is among the people and in savings-banks and trust companies not less than $200,000,000 of currency idle. Nothing but the best of security will tempt it from its hiding-places; but, that security offered, it can be had for a less rate of interest than ever before. Capital met its periodical shock in September, 1873, and great masses of it, some say one thousand millions, vanished as a dream, and are now represented by worthless bonds, bills, notes, and certificates of stock, worth but little more than the paper on which they are printed. This panic came upon us when the paper god was lord of the ascendant, when corner lots, at fictitious prices, were the par of exchange; when unproductive railroads were the El Dorados of visionaries, and wild schemes of improvement, both in this city and in all the cities of the Union, increased municipal debts to an unexampled degree. This reckless inflation of credits collapsed long before this law was passed. Money, the agent of capital, and, when idle, capital itself, was hoarded, and still remains inactive, or is loaned on call or unquestioned security. *This* is the contraction of which so many complain. It is not caused by the resumption act, but by a want of confidence in investments that offer. Confidence cannot be restored by a repeal or by issuing more paper money. But the occasion does offer you an opportunity of withdrawing a portion of this idle money, and thus reaching a specie standard. The banks can freely surrender a portion of their circulation, and thus be strong for resumption; while frightened and timid capital will gladly float into United States bonds when sold by the banks. Nothing is wanted but confidence, faith, and time to secure the closing triumph of our war policy by the redemption of the only promise we then made that has not been honestly redeemed.

EFFECT UPON EXISTING DEBTS.

The remaining objection to the law is that it will add to the burden of existing debts. This objection is also inseparable from any plan of resumption. Postponement or repeal will not help the matter. *The time for redemption must come.* Current indebtedness was never less than now. Liquidation has gone on rapidly since the panic, and in many cases by open bankruptcy. Debts contracted since the passage of the act have been made in view of resumption in 1879. Many of the old debts run for a long period of years, and when issued were made upon the presumption of specie payments before they matured. Other large masses of debts stipulate for the payment of both principal and interest in coin. Nearly all the best investment securities are now at or near par in gold and are bought and sold at gold values. Current debts in trade mature and are paid long before the time for resumption, and if renewed, the debtor and creditor adjust the mode of payment. All new transactions are based upon the knowledge that specie payments will come at the time stated, and for that reason lower rates of interest are stipulated for. Let it once be fixed in the public mind that on the 1st of January, 1879, paper money will be advanced to the specie standard, and debtors will readily borrow money payable in that standard at lower rates of interest. Capital will no longer be invested in gold bonds from the fear that if loaned to individuals it will be paid back in depreciated paper, but will eagerly be invested at low rates of interest on mortgage or other security if to be paid in improved and improving currency. Industries now languid or suspended will hopefully revive now that stocks are reduced, and productions will have a fixed commercial value, not only in home markets but the markets of the world. Merchants now fear the shrinkage of prices, but their stocks will be renewed at a corresponding reduction of prices until all are measured by the gold standard, when they need have no fear of change of prices except those arising from demand and supply. Debtors are also generally creditors, and the loss and gain in values will balance each other, and the time is ample in which all losses can be adjusted. Never could our condition be better to resume the specie standard than now, unless we intend to perpetuate the use of depreciated paper money and totally disregard the pledge of the public faith to redeem United States notes in coin.

THE DRIFTING PROCESS.

There are two objections made to the law which I ought not to pass over without reply. One is, that this law is forced resumption; that it is better to drift into resumption. It will come, they say, by natural causes. The other objection is that the law has been in force a year and we are no nearer resumption. It is therefore a dead-letter, and ought to be repealed. These two objections are not consistent with each other, but each has its believers, and should be answered.

The drifting process has been tried since 1868. Then the law fixed the volume of United States notes at $356,000,000, and forbade its contraction, and the amount of bank-notes at $300,000,000, and forbade its enlargement. It was said we would grow into resumption. This was the plausible dogma with which I was met when I sought the funding of notes into bonds. The result I have already stated. In 1870 the sectional inequality of the distribution of bank currency, inflamed into a passion by the sectional appeals of Horatio Seymour when a candidate for President in 1868, forced the enlargement of the limit of bank notes to $354,000,000; and the vain hope of stopping a panic by paper promises forced the enlargement of the limit of United States notes to $382,000,000. So will it always be with this drifting process. When we reach a specie standard it is safe enough. If national banks then issue more money, upon sufficient security to pay in coin, they do it at their peril, and the people cannot lose nor their standard of value fluctuate. But even if it was possible to fix the present volume of currency as an arbitrary limit, it would only prolong indefinitely the evils of a depreciated currency. No one believes that we could maintain in circulation near $800,000,000 of paper money all the time at par in gold. It must have the quality of flexibility in amount to meet the currents of trade and business—at times withdrawn, and when needed reissued, but always of the value of gold—and these qualities can only be secured by prompt redemption when it is not needed, and its reissue through loans and discounts by banks when the crops are to be moved or trade becomes active.

WHY NO APPARENT RESULTS.

And as to the objection that the law has not already produced more immediate results, I admit that this is an objection to the law, but it was unavoidable under the circumstances. The time for resumption should have been fixed much earlier, so that its effect would have been more rapid. If by the law the banks had been compelled to prepare for resumption sooner, the appreciation of our notes would have been more marked; and so if a portion of the notes could be funded, or either gold or notes could be held in reserve by the sale of bonds. Who does not wish that our notes were now worth ninety-five instead of eighty-nine cents on the dollar? And yet to produce that result we must have hastened either the day for resumption or strengthened the measures for resumption. But what is the remedy for this slow process? Is it to repeal the law, not a single provision of which by its terms has been put in full operation? Is it to revoke our promise and all efforts to fulfill it? Obviously not, but to stand by our engagement and perform it *sooner* if circumstances will allow.

CAN WE REDEEM ON THE 1ST DAY OF JANUARY, 1879?

And now, sir, I come to the second proposition stated: Can we resume specie payments on the 1st day of January, 1879?

On this proposition we are to consider the question as it affects the national banks, the fractional currency, and the United States notes.

NATIONAL CURRENCY.

As to the national banks, I have already stated how redemption with them becomes an easy and natural process to be performed without injury to them, or to their customers, or to their usefulness, by a transfer or sale of United States bonds especially set aside for that purpose, and only to the extent that each bank may deem essential to its safety. The national banks are now exceptionally strong. Their circulating notes amount to $346,479,756. Of these notes they have in their vaults the sum of $17,166,190. They have with the Treasurer of the United States $356,680,150 in United States bonds, worth $427,947,224 in currency or $374,582,200 in coin. They also hold United States bonds to secure United States deposits $13,981,500, and other United States bonds held in their vaults to the amount of $16,909,550. They have a surplus over and above the capital fully paid up, the sum of $192,300,000. With the great body of them the redemption of the whole or a large part of their circulation is a matter of indifference. To the extent of a certain per cent. of their deposits and 5 per cent. of their circulation they must maintain a reserve of United States notes, and to that extent will aid the United States in maintaining resumption. The amount of this reserve now required is $80,135,200, but the amount in hand is $118,800,987. As

United States notes are equivalent to coin with them, they will seek to hold as much as they can, as other banks in England hold the notes of the Bank of England. Is it not, then, apparent that the national banks are able to resume, are prepared to resume, and that resumption by them need not be delayed a single year; and that so far as their notes are concerned it is a shame and scandal that they are only worth eighty-nine cents on the dollar—and all because the United States will not advance its notes to par in gold?

FRACTIONAL CURRENCY.

Now, sir, as to the fractional currency. This was issued to take the place of the subsidiary silver coins of the country during the war. The amount outstanding, as shown by the books of the Treasury, is $45,120,132; but of this many millions have been lost and destroyed, and this is shown by the large amount of the old issues never presented although long superseded. It is probable that not exceeding $40,000,000 will be presented for redemption. Now, sir, as to this currency we are able to-day to issue silver coin of legal weight and fineness in exchange dollar for dollar for fractional currency, not only without loss but with an actual profit. One ounce of silver bullion, or four hundred and eighty grains of standard fineness, is worth in the market $1.05 in coin. One dollar of our silver coin contains three hundred and eighty four grains of standard silver; so that one dollar of silver coin will cost the United States eighty-four and one-quarter cents besides the cost of coining. To the extent that our people will take silver coin in exchange for fractional currency, the problem is already solved. It is said this coin will be hoarded. So much the better. We can furnish from our own mines all that is needed to the extent of fifteen millions on hand and two millions a month more, that being the extent of our coinage facilities. It is said it will be exported. No such good luck will befall us, for silver bullion is cheaper and better for export. If we issue it, we will either redeem a note or save paying out a note, and either way we make a profit. If fifty millions silver coin is held by our people it is to that extent a reserve for specie payments where it is most useful among the people. I wish they would take one hundred millions, and no doubt enough will be taken to redeem all the fractional currency that our people will not prefer to hold.

UNITED STATES NOTES.

And now the only remaining question is, Can we redeem or maintain at par by the 1st day of January, 1879, the United States notes?

The amount of them outstanding to-day is $370,943,392 less those lost and destroyed. Now, many who fear resumption suppose the whole mass of United States notes will then be presented for the gold; and they have counted up the number of tons of gold that will be required to do it. They figure up the interest at 5 per cent. on the whole sum, and state that as an addition to our annual interest account. It is not necessary to reply to such exaggerations; nor is it possible to state with precision what amount of United States notes would circulate at par in coin. They could then be made receivable for customs dues without a violation of the public faith. They will always be the reserve of national banks. They could then be made receivable for bonds of the United States. They could be supported by the power to sell bonds to redeem them. They would, as a matter of course, be supported by the whole gold reserve in the Treasury. They would take the place of certificates of deposit and be used in clearing-house exchanges.

Now, sir, with all these advantages, with the growing wealth and credit of our country, I do not believe the present volume of United States notes need be largely if any reduced to keep them at par in coin. We have now a gold balance in the Treasury of $37,120,772.73, and a currency balance of $9,529,404 over and above our currency and coin certificates. It is true this balance is subject to overdue and accruing demands fully stated in a recent letter of the Secretary of the Treasury, but a certain amount of these demands always remain uncalled for, and when presented are met by accruing revenue. Suppose (what I regard as an extreme case) that we add to this reserve $100,000,000, fifty million in coin certificates and fifty million in coin, does anybody doubt but it will be ample to redeem any note that is presented? Confidence being once established in their redemption, and who will want the gold for them? They can be and no doubt will be re-issued without or with the legal-tender clause, as the law may hereafter provide, and with their credit secured, established at par in coin, they will not only circulate in Texas and on the Pacific slope as well as in other parts of the United States, but, like the Bank of England note, in all countries that have commercial relations with us.

BURDEN OF RESUMPTION.

Let us pursue the argument taking the full burden of resumption as the interest of one hundred millions per annum. The rate of interest now in currency may be stated at 4 per cent. or 4½ per cent. in gold. Thus four to four and one-half millions a year three years hence is the extreme burden of specie payments. Sir, the sinking fund in three years amounts to more than the one hundred millions you are to keep in reserve. The saving already made thus far by funding the debt into 5 per cent. bonds is five millions a year. The saving that you will make by the funding into 4½ per cent. will be seven and one-half millions in gold, or nearly twice as much as is needed. The saving of four millions on the appropriation bills sent to us will cover the cost. A duty of five cents on the gallon of whisky will do it. One-half of the smallest duty ever levied on tea and coffee will do it. One-half of the taxes now levied on national banks by the United States will do it. The increased value of our tax on whisky and tobacco being paid in coin will twice do it. Are we able to do it? Are we able to keep our promises when made specific as to time, place, and manner? I do not care to discuss this question further. Sir, the United States has been blessed by divine Providence with all the gifts which He has ever showered upon the human race. We have a broad and fruitful land, with almost every variety of climate and production. We have forty millions of free people, industrious, intelligent, brave as becomes men, shrewd and sagacious in trade and production, and loving honor and a good name. To say that we cannot redeem our promises is to dishonor the blessings of God; it is to eat of the forbidden fruit when all the productions of nature and art are within our reach; it is to dishonor our name and credit when the world is ready to lend us at a less rate of interest than any nation of the world except Great Britain has ever borrowed for; it is a party retreat; it is a national retreat; it is a retreat of cowardice from a task we promised to perform, that we are able to perform, and which every noble motive that actuates mankind impels us to perform.

But, it is said, where is the gold to come from to enable us to resume. Not only is the gold of the world open to our competition, but we are the largest gold and silver producing country of the world.

The product of our mines is about one hundred millions a year, and a single year's product would more than enable us to resume. Our facilities for accumulating gold are greater than any other nation. "But the gold is exported." So it is, because we will not use it as the other nations do. Give it occupation here and it will remain here, and the products of our farms and workshops will be exported instead. It is said we can make a standard of something else that is not exportable. So we can by cutting ourselves off from the civilization of the human race.

Sir, I have been struck by the absolute poverty of invention of those who in our day seek to dispense with the gold standard. Every plan proposed, every idea suggested is but the repetition of plans and ideas proposed in the American colonies, in Great Britain, in China, and by George Law. Their schemes have been tried and exploded over and over again for four thousand years, and yet gold and silver now measure ever article of property and will measure the daily fluctuations of the contrivances they invent.

POWERS CONFERRED BY ACT OF 1875.

And now, sir, let us turn from the main question and briefly examine the third question: Are the agencies and measures prescribed by the act of 1875 sufficient for the purpose?

I need not remind this Senate and Senators around me how reluctantly I came to the support of this bill, because it does not contain provisions that for years I have struggled to secure. Still, sir, I feel bound to say that it contains ample agencies and powers to carry it into a full execution without the addition of a single provision by Congress. The first section of the bill is limited to the redemption of fractional currency. This, as I have shown, can now be fully executed, and the only criticism is that it has not been sooner executed. Not only can the notes be redeemed in silver without loss, but the actual cost of coining the silver, strange as it may seem, is less than the printing of the fractional currency.

COST OF SILVER COIN AND FRACTIONAL CURRENCY.

The cost of coining subsidiary silver coinage is shown by the Director of the Mint to be from 1½ to 2 per cent., and with the mints running to their full capacity it is much less.

The actual profits of seignorage will not only pay this cost, but more than the interest on the bonds we may sell to procure the bullion.

On the other hand, the cost of the fractional currency is 3½ per cent. of the amount issued; or, to be exact, the expense of preparing and redeeming the fractional currency for the year 1875 was $1,410,746.95. The amount issued was $40,365,145. And what is worse, the average life of these notes is less than one year, so that this expense is an annual one almost equal to the interest on the whole sum. Thus the stopping of the issue of fractional currency will save us $1,400,000. The silver coin pays a debt when issued, while the fractional currency only renews it, and it must be replaced by another note within a year. Sir, the wisdom of this provision is now so demonstrated that a committee of the House unanimously refuse to print the currency and demand the issue of the silver coin, while two months ago the scheme was pronounced visionary, impracticable, a sham. We are now at a specie basis for our fractional currency; and yet when the law passed we were told it would be hoarded, bought up by money-changers, exported. We are now told "Nobody wants the silver; they prefer the fractional notes." So it is and so it will be when we approach the gold standard. Nobody will want to give up the United States notes for gold as soon as the note will buy as much as gold.

But it is said we can only buy the silver bullion by issuing bonds. That is true now, because our surplus revenue is not large; but how will the United States ever pay its notes at a cheaper rate. One million of dollars of 5 per cent. bonds will to-day buy sufficient silver bullion to make $1,200,000 in subsidiary silver coin. When and how can this operation of paying our debts be better commenced, unless we mean to postpone payment indefinitely. It has been said that the 5 per cent. bonds authorized have been exhausted. Not so. The law is plain and express, and was so designed and intended, to authorize the Secretary of the Treasury not only to use any surplus revenue, but "to issue, sell, and dispose of at not less than par in coin either of the *descriptions* of bonds of the United States described in the act" for refunding the public debt. The refunding act is only referred to for the "description" of the bonds authorized. But to make this construction more clear, it is provided "that all provisions of law inconsistent with this act are hereby repealed." Thus, not only the public faith but all the surplus revenue and the public credit, as represented by either of three kinds of bonds, to wit, those bearing 4, 4½, and 5 per cent. interest in gold, is granted to the Secretary to enable him to execute this trust. The only limit in amount is the amount that will enable him to execute the law. The only limit of price at which he can sell the bonds, is "not less than par in coin."

The second section is only material as it tends to induce the coining of gold by repealing the mint charge.

So much of the third section as relates to national banks is not material except as it provides a way by which circulating notes may be issued; but if issued it will be with full knowledge that in due time they must be redeemed in coin at the pleasure of the holder.

Then comes the provision—the vital provision—of the law: "And on and after the 1st day of January, A. D. 1879, the Secretary of the Treasury shall redeem in coin the United States legal-tender notes then outstanding on their presentation for redemption." Then follows the ample power already quoted: "And to enable the Secretary of the Treasury to prepare and provide for the redemption in this act authorized or required, he is authorized to use any surplus revenue from time to time in the Treasury not otherwise appropriated, and to issue, sell, and dispose of," at not less than par in coin, either of the bonds already referred to. Such are the duties enjoined, and such are the powers conferred.

Sir, in this respect, both the powers and duties of this act are clearer and stronger than in the acts under which Great Britain resumed and France is now resuming. Who can doubt that with or without further legislation the work can be accomplished by a Secretary who will obey and execute the law? The power to "prepare" for resumption is a broad discretion that commences with the passage of the act and continues during every hour and day of its existence, but is one to be exercised with exceeding caution and moderation.

AUXILIARY LEGISLATION.

But, sir, this is not all. When Congress passes an act imposing a duty upon a public officer, it implies an obligation that it will furnish all the aid and auxiliary legislation necessary to carry it into execution. The extent and nature of this is within the discretion of Congress, but when the power conferred upon him is ample, and the duty imposed is clear, he must act even though Congress neglect its duty to support him by auxiliary legislation.

And this brings me to the last proposition I propose to discuss, and that is—

What additional legislation ought Congress now to adopt in aid of the law?

The Secretary of the Treasury recommends first that the legal-tender quality of the United States note be taken from it before 1879. I cannot agree to this, for the United States note is as much a contract to pay money as a bond, and we cannot take from that note any quality that gives it value until we are prepared to redeem it in coin. The proposition is too much like the act of March, 1863, already referred to, which stripped the note of its quality of convertibility into bonds.

His second recommendation is—

That authority be given for funding legal-tender notes into bonds bearing a low rate of interest. * * * It seems probable that a bond bearing interest at the rate of 4 per cent. would invite the funding of a sufficient amount of legal-tender notes to lessen materially the sum of gold which, in the absence of such provision, must be accumulated in the Treasury by the 1st of January, 1879, to carry out the imperative requirements of the act of January 14, 1875. If it be apprehended that authority to the Secretary to fund an unlimited amount of notes might lead to too sudden contraction of the currency, Congress could limit the amount to be funded in any given period of time. The process being in no sense compulsory as to the holders of United States notes, and the rate of interest on the bonds being made low, it is not probable that currency which could find profitable employment would be presented for redemption in such bonds. Only the excess of notes above the needs of business would seek such conversion. Authority to the Secretary of the Treasury to redeem and cancel two million of legal-tender notes per month by this process would greatly facilitate redemption at the time now fixed by law, and besides would have the advantage of publicity as to the exact amount to be withdrawn in any given month. Bonds issued for this purpose should be of the denomination of fifty and one hundred dollars, and any multiple thereof, in order to meet the convenience of all classes of holders of United States notes.

The President in his annual message recommends—

That the Secretary of the Treasury be authorized to redeem, say, not to exceed $2,000,000 monthly of legal-tender notes, by issuing in their stead a long bond, bearing interest at the rate of 3.65 per cent. per annum, of denominations ranging from $50 to $1,000 each. This would in time reduce the legal-tender notes to a volume that could be kept afloat without demanding redemption in large sums suddenly.

Third. That additional power be given to the Secretary of the Treasury to accumulate gold for final redemption, either by increasing revenue, curtailing expenses, or both—it is preferable to do both; and I recommend that reduction of expenditures be made wherever it can be done without impairing Government obligations or crippling the due execution thereof.

These recommendations substantially concurring are wise and would be efficient, and to secure them ample means are provided by the application of the sinking fund for two or three years without additional taxation. Indeed it is neither wise or prudent to apply the sinking fund to the purchase of bonds not due, at a high premium, when it may be applied according to the act creating it to the purchase of notes already due.

The honorable Senator from Vermont [Mr. Morrill] has introduced a bill, and a number of other bills and propositions have been referred to the Committee on Finance; and the elaborate resolutions of the Chamber of Commere of New York are now before us.

I will not anticipate the provisions of these various propositions, except so fár as to say that I will cheerfully support any measure of wise economy proposed to strengthen the public Treasury; that I will cheerfully vote for a moderate tax on tea and coffee, because this will increase our revenue without adding to the cost of the articles, and be the means of enabling us to repeal other taxes that are both a burden and an inconvenience, and will also strengthen the Treasury;

that I will gladly vote for the voluntary conversion of a limited amount of United States notes into bonds, as each of those measures will tend to "prepare" us for a specie standard. But, sir, each of these measures, and others that may be proper, are not, in my judgment, indispensable to the full and complete execution of the law of 1875 on or before the 1st day of January, 1879.

Indeed it may well be questioned whether all of them may not be properly postponed until the next session, when the deliberate judgment of Congress, guided by the sense of the people, can be rendered. I will gladly vote for them now, but we have acted together thus far and I will not unduly press upon my associates measures they do not fully approve.

Sir, I have a confident belief that if Congress will now hold fast to the law as it stands, the drift of events and the practical operation of the law will not only vindicate its wisdom, but will secure in due time every proper auxiliary legislation to carry it into full execution. The duty of the hour demands firmness and faith. There are times in the lives of nations and individuals when the temptation is strong to turn from the path of honor, to shrink from and evade the performance of obligations. Then it is more than ever that the old adage should be remembered that "honesty is the best policy." For one I feel that my course is as clear as the sunlight of heaven; and I trust that the great party to which I belong may now, as in sterner times and under greater difficulties, stand fast to the national honor pledged by it in the act of 1875; and when the difficulties inseparable from a great duty have passed away, we will be as proud of our position now as we are of the firmness and faith with which we prosecuted a great war, and secured to the people of our day and of future generations the blessings of national union and universal liberty.

I move that the memorial of the New York Chamber of Commerce be referred to the Committee on Finance.

The motion was agreed to.

○

www.ingramcontent.com/pod-product-compliance
Lightning Source LLC
LaVergne TN
LVHW011132110826
845150LV00008B/2306

* 9 7 8 1 4 1 8 1 9 4 9 5 6 *